Nuts

Rio Nuevo Publishers®
P.O. Box 5250, Tucson, Arizona 85703-0250
(520) 623-9558, www.rionuevo.com

Text and photography © 2006 by Rio Nuevo Publishers. Food
styling by Tracy Vega. Many thanks to Nan Stockholm Walden and
the Green Valley Pecan Company for providing beautiful nuts, and
to Connie Choza for providing a perfect setting for the photo
shoots for this book.

Photography credits as follows:
Katie Cline: page 27. W. Ross Humphreys: Front cover, pages 3, 5, 12,
43, 56, 63, 66, 69, 80. Robin Stancliff: Back cover, pages 4, 19, 20, 31,
39, 44, 49, 55, 61.

Library of Congress Cataloging-in-Publication Data
Grimes, Gwin Grogan.
Nuts : pistachio, pecan & piñon / Gwin Grogan Grimes.
    p. cm. — (Cook West series)
Includes index.
ISBN-13: 978-1-887896-87-0
ISBN-10: 1-887896-87-2
1. Cookery (Nuts) 2. Pistachio. 3. Pecan. 4. Pine nuts. I. Title. II.
Title: Pistachio, pecan & piñon.
TX814.G755 2006
641.6'45—dc22

                                        2006020401

Design: Karen Schober, Seattle, Washington.
Printed in Korea.
10 9 8 7 6 5 4 3 2 1

nuts
Pistachio, Pecan & Piñon

GWIN GROGAN GRIMES

≈COOK WEST≈
SERIES

RIO NUEVO PUBLISHERS
TUCSON, ARIZONA

contents

xxxxxx

introduction

Not only are pecans, pistachios, and piñons a tasty, nutritious snack right out of the shell or flavorful ingredients in many a dish, they are three important agricultural products of the Southwest region. I'll never forget the first time I saw pistachio orchards in southern New Mexico, on my way to Ruidoso—or the fantastic taste of the fresh and flavorful nuts sold in the shops nestled by the roadside. Growing up, I'd known of only two kinds—dyed red and natural—so green chile and garlic-roasted pistachios were a revelation.

I was much more familiar with pecans. I've never lived in a state that didn't grow pecans, and lots of them. My mother is the pecan connoisseur of the family, selecting the finest Stuarts over tiny "native" varieties. She says these make the best pralines, for which she has always been known. (I am dedicating this book to her, because she taught me very early on that the most important ingredient in any recipe is love.)

Fall and winter always have been pecan-shelling seasons in our family. My father, ever the handyman, enjoyed testing various nutcrackers. Since my mom required pristine halves for the pecan pralines, nutcrackers had to crack the shells without crushing the tender meat. Many hours were spent, trays on laps, shelling pecans in front of our favorite television shows.

I still regret that my first experience with the venerable piñon, also known as pinyon or pine nut, was not a good one. In the mid-1980s I was eager to try a new Italian sauce I'd read about called pesto. I found a tiny packet of *pignolis*, as the Italians call them, at the local supermarket. Unfortunately, their vintage was unknown, and my sauce was bitter due to the rancid nuts.

I learned a valuable lesson about buying fresh nuts and storing them in the freezer until needed, and fortunately the experience did not deter me from further experimentation with piñons. Now I use these buttery morsels in many dishes. When a friend recently brought back some very fresh, unshelled piñons from Mexico, I ate them all before they could find their way into a pasta or cookie.

I hope that you will enjoy cooking with pistachios, pecans, and piñons as much as I do. They are extremely versatile and healthful ingredients that will enhance your savory and sweet cuisine. May the following recipes inspire you to get cooking!

Tradition and Nutrition Pistachios, pecans, and piñons are the seeds of trees. They are delicious simply shelled and eaten out of hand, yet versatile enough to be used in a variety of ways in both savory and sweet recipes.

Pistachio trees may be native to southwestern Asia, but they are avidly cultivated in the Mediterranean region, Australia, and the southwestern United States. The fruit of the tree is a "nut" only in the culinary sense—botanically, it's a drupe. They are ripe when the shells split open, leading the Chinese to call the pistachio the "happy nut" and Middle Easterners to describe pistachios as "smiling." Pistachios are among the "elder statesmen" of the nut trees and were considered a valued gift in the Old Testament, coveted by the Queen of Sheba, and enjoyed as a delicacy by Roman aristocrats. Like most nuts, pistachios pack a vitamin and mineral punch. A one-ounce serving has more than 10 percent of the recommended daily allowance of fiber, vitamin B-6, thiamine, phosphorus, and copper. Pistachios also contain phytochemicals, which may help protect against some cancers, heart disease, and other chronic health conditions. They are among the best sources of antioxidants as well.

The pecan is the only major tree nut originally found in North America, and its nuts were used by Native Americans as early as the sixteenth century. Texas—where the pecan is the state tree—produces more native pecans than any other state, and is second only to Georgia in the production of hybrid, or orchard-grown, varieties. Unlike the piñon, which has only three major varieties found in the U.S., pecan varieties number more than 1,000 and come in sizes from midget to mammoth. Fiber-rich, cholesterol-free pecans provide more than nineteen vitamins and minerals. They contain a variety of phyto-chemicals and are an excellent source of protein.

The nut we commonly call the piñon comes primarily from the species of tree called *Pinus monophylla,* according to the USDA Forest Service. It grows across the western part of this country from southern Idaho, western Utah, northwestern Arizona, southwestern New Mexico, through most of Nevada (where it's the state tree), and into California. Piñon trees have more than just culinary value, also having provided fuel, medicine, and shelter to Native Americans for thousands of years. The piñon's oil is used in cosmetics and wood finishes. This nutritional powerhouse is made up of about 9.5 percent protein, 23 percent fat, and 54 percent carbohydrates, with 20 amino acids as well as vitamin A, thiamine, riboflavin, and niacin. Interestingly, piñons are comparable in nutritional value to pecans.

Equipment The recipes in this book were created and tested in a standard home kitchen—mine—with ordinary equipment. If you prefer to buy pecans in the shell, you'll need a good cracker. My father liked an "inertia"-style contraption that used rubber bands, but I still use a simple, spring-loaded gadget that resembles a tiny pair of tongs.

Otherwise, here are a couple of things I can't cook without: an instant-read thermometer and a pepper grinder (a $10 model from the discount store works just as well as a $100 fancy-schmancy mill). You need only three knives to do most culinary jobs: a chef's knife, a paring knife, and a serrated bread knife. That's all I used to prepare every dish in this book. That's it. You've got everything else you need: pots, skillet, baking sheet, spatula, and a wooden spoon or two. A couple of the recipes specify a stand mixer or food processor, but there's always a way around it if you don't own one.

Ingredients I'll start with the same point I make when I teach a cooking class: You cannot make a superior product from inferior ingredients. For the best results, use the best quality ingredients you can find. Note that I did not say the most expensive ingredients. The best cooks are the most discerning shoppers. Buy your nuts at a store with a lot of turnover in product. I am fortunate to have an excellent supplier, Vending Nut Co., in my hometown. They do mail order (www.vendingnut.com or 800-429-9260), but if you've got an in-town supplier, by all means support your local business!

Treat your ingredients with respect. For long-term storage, keep nuts well-wrapped in the freezer. Always taste the nuts before using them in a recipe. If they have developed off-flavors or don't taste fresh, feed them to the birds and squirrels and buy more.

Toasting Nuts Toast nuts when indicated in the recipe. Toasting brings out the rich flavor of nuts. Either bake in a 350-degree F oven for about 5 to 7 minutes, stirring occasionally; heat in a dry skillet on the stovetop over medium heat, stirring often, for about 5 minutes; or place on a microwave-safe plate and cook on medium heat in the microwave, stirring often, for 5 minutes. Watch carefully so the nuts don't burn. Burned nuts will ruin a dish, so toss them out and start over.

Prosciutto-Piñon Bruschetta

xxxxxx

This elegant appetizer is best served warm from the oven.

Serves 12

Preheat oven to 350 degrees F. Line 2 baking sheets with parchment paper or coat with cooking spray.

In a mixing bowl, cream the butter until light and fluffy. Stir in the prosciutto, cheese, and pepper.

Place the slices of bread on baking sheets. Toast in the preheated oven until light golden brown, about 10 minutes. Remove from the oven, turn over, and toast for another 5 minutes.

Spread each round with some of the butter mixture and sprinkle with piñons.

Cooking spray (optional)

2 sticks (1 cup) unsalted butter, softened

1 cup diced prosciutto

1 cup shredded Parmigiano-Reggiano cheese

1 teaspoon freshly ground pepper

2 baguettes, sliced into $1/_2$-inch-thick rounds

1 cup piñons, toasted (see page 11)

Bleu-Pistachio Cheese Spread

xxxxxx

Serves 10–12

8 ounces cream cheese, softened

8 ounces bleu cheese, such as Maytag, Cabrales, or Gorgonzola, crumbled

1/2 cup shredded mild white cheese, such as Monterey Jack or Oaxaca

2 tablespoons dry white wine

1/2 cup pistachios, toasted and chopped (see page 11)

1 teaspoon sweet paprika

Serve with crackers and crudités, or my favorite way: spooned onto spears of endive.

Place the cheeses and wine in a mixing bowl and fold together with a rubber spatula or wooden spoon until combined. Shape the mixture into a large ball or log. Sprinkle the pistachios and paprika onto a baking sheet and roll the cheese ball or log in them until thoroughly coated. Wrap the ball or log in plastic wrap and refrigerate until firm, at least 2 hours, before serving.

Cheddar-Pecan Slices

xxxxxx

Serves 8–10

1 1/2 cups shredded sharp Cheddar cheese

1/4 cup sour cream

1/4 cup toasted chopped pecans (see page 11)

It's amazing the flavors you can achieve with just a few simple ingredients. This is best served with an assortment of fresh fruit and crackers.

Place the cheese and sour cream in a mixing bowl and beat at medium speed until combined. Stir in the pecans. With a rubber spatula, scrape the mixture onto a sheet of plastic wrap. Use the wrap to help form the cheese into a log about 10 inches long. Cover completely with plastic and refrigerate until firm, at least 2 hours, before serving. Slice the log into 1/4-inch slices to serve.

Five-Spice Mixed Nuts

xxxxxx

When packed into pretty jars or simply wrapped in cellophane, these Asian-flavored piquant nuts make an excellent hostess gift or party favor. Or serve them with cocktails before dinner. If you can't find five-spice powder (a blend of Chinese cinnamon, black pepper, cloves, fennel seed, and star anise) in the supermarket, try your local Asian food market.

Preheat oven to 325 degrees F. Line a baking sheet with parchment paper or coat it with cooking spray.

In a large mixing bowl, stir together the butter, soy sauce, five-spice powder, garlic, ginger, and cayenne. Gently add the pecans and pistachios, and stir to coat. Spread the nuts evenly on the prepared baking sheet and place in the hot oven. Bake for 10 minutes, remove from the oven, and stir. Repeat until the nuts are toasty brown and mostly dry. Turn out onto a clean sheet of parchment paper or a clean baking sheet and let cool completely, separating the nuts.

Store in an airtight container.

Serves 16 or makes 4 gifts

Cooking spray (optional)

$1/2$ stick (4 tablespoons) unsalted butter, melted

2 tablespoons soy sauce

1 teaspoon five-spice powder

$1/2$ teaspoon granulated garlic

$1/2$ teaspoon ground ginger

$1/4$ teaspoon cayenne pepper

$1/2$ pound pecan halves

$1/2$ pound shelled pistachios

Sugared Pecans

xxxxxx

Serves 8

These are especially delicious served with cocktails or tossed into a green salad made with fresh baby spinach, red onion rings, and thinly sliced fresh pears.

Cooking spray (optional)

1/2 stick (4 tablespoons) unsalted butter, melted

1/4 cup dark brown sugar

1/4 teaspoon ground cinnamon

2 cups pecan halves

Preheat oven to 325 degrees F. Line a baking sheet with parchment paper or coat with cooking spray.

In a mixing bowl, stir together the melted butter, sugar, and cinnamon. Add the pecans and stir gently so as not to break the halves into smaller pieces. Spread onto the prepared baking sheet and place in the oven. Bake for 15–20 minutes, stirring often. Remove from the oven and let cool. Separate nuts and serve.

Tomato, Basil, and Piñon Salad Dressing

xxxxxx

Serves 6

This is excellent when tossed with mixed greens—or served over steamed vegetables such as green beans, new potatoes, or asparagus. Chop the basil right before adding it to the dressing to preserve its bright color.

1/2 cup balsamic vinegar

2 tablespoons water

Pinch of granulated sugar, or to taste

1 cup olive oil

1/2 cup sun-dried tomatoes packed in oil, chopped

1/2 cup piñons, toasted (see page 11)

1/2 cup fresh basil leaves

In a small mixing bowl, mix the vinegar, water, and sugar. Whisk in the olive oil in a steady stream until well blended. Stir in tomatoes and piñons. Roughly chop the basil leaves and add to the mixture. If you are making this ahead, cover and refrigerate for up to 8 hours. Mix well before serving.

Feta and Piñon Salad with Apples

xxxxxx

This unusual salad hints of the Mediterranean and is elegant enough for a dinner party.

In a salad bowl, whisk together the vinegar, oil, and mustard. Add the apple slices, tossing gently to coat with the dressing. Add the endive and toss. Season with salt and pepper, adjusting to taste. Garnish with feta and nuts and serve immediately.

Serves 6

$1/3$ cup sherry vinegar

$1/3$ cup canola oil

1 tablespoon Dijon mustard

1 medium apple, Granny Smith or Gala, cut into thin slices

1 pound Belgian endive, separated into leaves

Salt

Freshly ground pepper

$1/2$ cup crumbled feta cheese

$1/2$ cup piñons, toasted (see page 11)

Pistachio-Orange Salad

xxxxxx

Serves 6

¹/₂ pound fresh baby spinach

¹/₄ cup pecans, toasted and chopped (see page 11)

1 can (11 ounces) mandarin oranges, drained

¹/₂ cup orange crème yogurt

3 tablespoons mayonnaise

2–3 teaspoons white wine vinegar

Salt and freshly ground pepper

This colorful salad, bursting with fresh, bright flavors and accented with toasted pistachios, makes a light prelude to a rich meal.

In a salad bowl, toss the spinach, pecans, and oranges. In a small mixing bowl, stir together the yogurt and mayonnaise, adding just enough vinegar to thin the dressing. Season with salt and pepper to taste. Drizzle the dressing over the salad, then gently toss to evenly coat the spinach. Serve immediately.

Pear Salad with Glazed Pecans

xxxxxx

A great salad for fall, when pears are at their peak.

Serves 4

Line a baking sheet with parchment paper or coat thoroughly with cooking spray.

In a frying pan over medium-high heat, melt the butter. Add the sugar and pecan halves, stirring just to coat. Cook until the sugar melts, then reduce the heat to low. Stir and continue cooking until the sugar turns golden brown. Remove from heat and pour the nuts onto the prepared baking sheet. Let them cool, then separate into pieces. The pecans may be glazed ahead of time and stored in an airtight container.

In a salad bowl, combine the greens and pears. Drizzle on the vinaigrette and toss lightly to coat the lettuces and pears. Divide the salad onto four plates and garnish with glazed pecans.

Cooking spray (optional)

1 tablespoon unsalted butter

$1/4$ cup sugar

$1/2$ cup pecan halves

6 cups mixed baby lettuces or field greens

2 small ripe pears, thinly sliced

$2/3$ cup raspberry vinaigrette

Pecan-Stuffed Dates

xxxxxx

Serves 10

Cooking spray (optional)

10 slices bacon, preferably
applewood-smoked

30 pitted dates

30 pecan halves

This hot hors d'oeuvre will add a touch of elegance to any party. It may sound like a strange combination, but—trust me—these are divine!

Preheat oven to 400 degrees F. Line a baking pan with parchment paper or coat with cooking spray.

Cut each bacon slice into thirds. Stuff each date with a pecan half. Wrap a piece of bacon around each date, securing with a toothpick.

Place the dates on the prepared baking sheet and bake for 12–15 minutes, or until the bacon is crisp. Drain on paper towels and serve immediately.

Pistachio-Stuffed Mushrooms

xxxxxx

A classic party dish updated with bold, modern flavors.

Serves 4

Preheat oven to 350 degrees F. Line a baking sheet with parchment paper or coat with cooking spray.

Trim the mushroom stems from the caps and scrape the gills, leaving a hollow in the cap. Mince the stems. In a large frying pan, melt the butter and sauté the minced stems, onion, and pistachios until the mushrooms and onion are tender. With a slotted spoon, remove from the pan and place in a mixing bowl. Add the bread crumbs, parsley, salt, pepper, and paprika. Taste and adjust seasonings.

In the frying pan, place the mushroom caps, top side down, in a single layer (you may have to cook these in batches). Gently sauté until the mushrooms release some of their water, but not until they are limp.

Place the mushroom caps on the prepared baking sheet. Stuff each cap with the onion-nut mixture and bake for about 15 minutes, or until the mushrooms are hot and tender. Serve immediately.

Cooking spray (optional)

16 large button mushrooms

$3/4$ stick (6 tablespoons) unsalted butter

$1/2$ onion, minced

$1/4$ cup pistachios, toasted and chopped (see page 11)

$1/3$ cup unseasoned bread crumbs

2 tablespoons chopped flat-leaf parsley

$1/4$ teaspoon salt

$1/4$ teaspoon freshly ground pepper

$1/4$ teaspoon smoked paprika

Pesto Spirals

xxxxxx

Serves 8–10

2 sheets frozen puff pastry, thawed overnight in refrigerator

1 cup fresh basil leaves

3 tablespoons piñons

4 cloves garlic

$^1/_4$–$^1/_2$ cup extra-virgin olive oil

$^1/_2$ cup shredded Parmigiano-Reggiano cheese

Cooking spray (optional)

Prepared puff pastry sheets, found in the freezer section of supermarkets, are spread with pesto and then rolled and sliced into little spirals.

Remove the package of puff pastry from the refrigerator. Unwrap and unfold the sheets, flattening the seams with your fingers. Set aside.

Put the basil, piñons, and garlic in a food processor fitted with a metal blade. Pulse several times until all the ingredients are chopped finely and evenly. With the blade running, drizzle in a stream of olive oil until a smooth paste is formed. Add the cheese, pulsing a few times until the mixture is blended. It should be a bit thicker than the pesto used to sauce pasta. If needed, add a bit more olive oil, a little at a time, until the pesto is easy to spread.

With a pastry brush, spread a thin, even layer of pesto over each sheet of puff pastry, leaving about a ¼-inch border on one narrow end.

One at a time, roll up each sheet like a jellyroll. When you get to the end, dampen the end with a bit of water and seal the roll closed by slightly pinching the seam.

Wrap each roll in plastic wrap and refrigerate for about an hour to firm up the pastry. To make ahead of time and freeze, insert the wrapped rolls into a freezer storage bag and place in the freezer.

Preheat oven to 425 degrees F.

Prepare 2 baking sheets by lining them with parchment paper or coating them with cooking spray.

Slice the puff-pastry–pesto rolls into ¼-inch slices and lay the slices on a prepared baking sheet so the spiral faces up.

Bake for about 15–20 minutes, or until the pastry is puffed and lightly golden brown. Gently remove from the baking sheets with a thin metal spatula and let cool on wire racks or serve warm.

If you are baking the spirals earlier on the day that you plan to serve them, do not refrigerate the baked pastries, or they may become soggy. Cover them with a clean dish towel. When you are ready to serve, remove the towel and return the spirals to a warm oven to re-heat for a few minutes.

Cranberry-Pecan Spread

xxxxxx

Serves 6

8 ounces cream cheese, softened

$1/4$ cup orange juice concentrate, thawed

$1/2$ cup toasted chopped pecans (see page 11)

$1/2$ cup dried cranberries, chopped

This makes a lovely gift when accompanied by a loaf of home-made banana bread. You can also serve this on toast or bagels. Or for a cocktail snack, serve with gourmet crackers.

Place the cream cheese and juice in a mixing bowl. With an electric mixer, beat at medium speed until the cream cheese is light and fluffy. Stir in the pecans and cranberries. Cover and refrigerate to allow the flavors to blend and mellow, at least 1 hour.

Maple-Pecan Chicken Breasts

xxxxxx

Serves 4

Two trees contribute to the flavor of this chicken dish. The maple adds sweetness and the pecans, crunch.

1 cup chopped pecans

3 tablespoons all-purpose flour

1 teaspoon salt

4 skinless, boneless chicken breasts

2 tablespoons maple syrup

2 tablespoons unsalted butter

2 or more tablespoons canola or vegetable oil, as needed

In a baking dish, stir together the pecans, flour, and salt. Coat the chicken breasts with the maple syrup, then place in the baking dish. Pat the pecan mixture evenly onto the chicken breasts.

Melt the butter and oil together in a large frying pan over medium-high heat. Add the chicken breasts in one layer and cook for about 10 minutes. Turn over each breast with a pair of tongs and cook for another 5 minutes, or until the chicken is browned and an instant-read thermometer inserted into the thickest part of a breast reads 165 degrees F.

Baked Honey-Pistachio Chicken

xxxxxx

Pistachios, which are native to Persia, thrive in the Mediterranean as well as in the American Southwest. Try to seek out locally produced honeys whenever you can—the farmers market is usually a good place to find them.

Preheat oven to 375 degrees F. Coat a 9 x 13-inch baking pan with cooking spray.

In one shallow dish, whisk together the eggs and honey. In another shallow dish, mix the pistachios, bread crumbs, oregano, salt, and pepper.

Dip each chicken breast first in the egg mixture, then in the nut mixture, making sure to coat them evenly. Arrange the breasts in a single layer in the prepared baking dish and drizzle the melted butter over the top.

Bake the chicken for about 40 minutes, or until an instant-read thermometer inserted into the thickest part of the breast reads 165 degrees F.

Serves 6

Cooking spray

2 eggs

$1/2$ cup honey

1 cup finely chopped pistachios

1 cup unseasoned bread crumbs

2 teaspoons fresh oregano, or 1 teaspoon dried

$1/2$ teaspoon salt

1 teaspoon freshly ground pepper

6 bone-in chicken breast halves

$1/2$ stick (4 tablespoons) unsalted butter, melted

Pasta with Chicken and Piñons

xxxxxx

Serves 4

This quick pasta dish can be made even faster with leftover roast chicken.

1/2 stick (4 tablespoons) unsalted butter

1/4 cup piñons

1 cup sun-dried tomatoes packed in oil, drained and chopped

1 1/2 cups heavy (whipping) cream

1/4 cup cognac

1 pound fettuccine or linguine

3/4 pound smoked chicken breast, chopped

Melt the butter in a frying pan over medium heat. Add the piñons and sauté for about 5 minutes. Add the tomatoes and cook for another 2 minutes.

Add the cream and cognac to the pan and cook, stirring often, until the sauce is thickened, about 15 minutes.

Meanwhile, cook the pasta until al dente by following the package directions. The water you cook your pasta in should be "as salty as the sea."

Add the chicken to the sauce and heat through. Drain the pasta, reserving about 2–3 tablespoons of the cooking water. Add the pasta to the sauce and toss to coat thoroughly. Add a little of the pasta cooking water if necessary to thin the sauce and coat the pasta evenly.

Toasted Pecan and Asparagus Pasta

xxxxxx

Serves 4

1 pound fresh asparagus, trimmed and cut into 2-inch pieces

2 tablespoons unsalted butter

2 cloves garlic, minced

1/2 pound button mushrooms, sliced

2 tablespoons chopped fresh chives or flat-leaf parsley

1 tablespoon lemon juice

1 teaspoon salt

1/2 teaspoon ground white pepper

4 tablespoons toasted chopped pecans (see page 11)

1/2 cup heavy (whipping) cream

1 pound dried or fresh linguine, fettuccine, or spaghetti, cooked and drained (reserve 1/4 cup of cooking water)

Additional chopped fresh chives or flat-leaf parsley, for garnish (optional)

To trim asparagus, snap off the ends. They will naturally break off where the tough, woody part of the stem begins.

Boil about 1½ quarts of water in a 2-quart saucepan and add the asparagus. Cook for about 2 minutes, then drain off the water and set aside.

In a large skillet, melt the butter over medium-high heat. Add the garlic and cook for about 2 minutes. Add the mushrooms and cook, stirring frequently, for another 5 minutes or until the mushrooms have shed their water and it has evaporated from the pan. To the pan, add the reserved asparagus, chives or parsley, lemon juice, salt, pepper, pecans, and cream. Cook until heated through, about 2–3 minutes. Add the pasta and toss to thoroughly coat the noodles, adding some of the reserved pasta cooking water, if needed, to thin the sauce. Garnish with chives or flat-leaf parsley, if desired, and serve.

Pesto Sauce

xxxxxx

When using this pesto as a pasta sauce, reserve about ¼ cup of the pasta cooking water to use to thin the sauce, if necessary, and to help make it adhere to the pasta. Also delicious on grilled or roasted meat.

Wash the basil leaves and pat dry with paper towels. Put the basil, piñons, and garlic in a food processor fitted with a metal blade. Pulse several times until the ingredients are chopped finely and evenly, scraping down with a flexible spatula when necessary. With the machine running, drizzle in a stream of olive oil until a smooth paste is formed. Add the cheese, salt, and pepper, pulsing a few times until the mixture is well blended. Taste and adjust the seasonings.

Makes about 2 cups

2 cups fresh basil leaves

¹/₂ cup piñons

6 cloves garlic

1 cup extra-virgin olive oil

1 cup shredded Parmigiano-Reggiano cheese

¹/₂ teaspoon salt

1 teaspoon freshly ground pepper

Turkey Breast Stuffed with Dried Fruit and Piñons

xxxxxx

Serves 4

Cooking spray (optional)

1/2 cup piñons

1/2 cup raisins

1/3 cup chopped dried apricots

1 boneless turkey breast, about 3 pounds

1/2 teaspoon salt

1 teaspoon freshly ground pepper

1 teaspoon fresh thyme leaves or 1/2 teaspoon dried thyme

1 cup sliced onions

1 cup sliced carrots

1 cup chopped celery

1 stick (1/2 cup) unsalted butter, melted

1/2 cup orange juice

This is a nice holiday dish for small family gatherings. It is worthwhile to seek out the dried apricots from California. They are a bit darker than the Mediterranean ones and have a lot more flavor.

Preheat the oven to 350 degrees F.

Coat a roasting pan with cooking spray or line it with aluminum foil.

In a small bowl, mix the piñons, raisins, and apricots.

With a sharp paring knife, make a lengthwise incision on one side of the turkey breast and slice three-quarters of the way to the other side to create a pocket inside the breast. Stuff with the fruit and nut mixture, securing the opening with a couple of toothpicks.

Season the outside of the turkey breast with salt, pepper, and thyme.

Add the onions, carrots, and celery to the roasting pan and set the turkey breast on top. In a small bowl, mix the melted butter and orange juice. Baste the turkey with this mixture. Cover the roasting pan with a lid or aluminum foil.

Bake the turkey for 1 hour. Remove the lid or foil from pan and baste again with the butter-orange juice mixture. Bake for another 15 minutes, uncovered, basting every 5 minutes, or until the turkey is golden brown and an instant-read thermometer inserted into the meat registers 155 degrees F. Remove from the oven and let it cool for 10 minutes before slicing. Serve with the roasted vegetables.

Beef Tenderloin with Piñon Stuffing
xxxxxx

If beef tenderloin is out of your price range, try this stuffing with pork loin.

Serves 6–8

Cooking spray (optional)

¹/₂ cup olive oil, divided

¹/₂ cup piñons

¹/₄ cup finely chopped yellow or white onion

3 shallots, finely chopped

2 cloves garlic, finely chopped

¹/₂ cup sun-dried tomatoes packed in oil, drained and chopped

1¹/₂ cups unseasoned bread crumbs

¹/₂ cup chopped fresh flat-leaf parsley

¹/₂ teaspoon salt, plus additional for the roast

1 teaspoon freshly ground pepper, plus additional for the roast

1 beef tenderloin, about 3 pounds

Preheat the oven to 425 degrees F.

Coat a roasting pan large enough for the tenderloin with cooking spray or line it with aluminum foil.

Heat about 3 tablespoons of olive oil in a medium frying pan over medium heat. Add piñons and cook until golden brown, about 3–4 minutes. Remove nuts with a slotted spoon and set aside.

Place the onion and shallots in the pan and sauté until the vegetables are clear and tender, about 5 minutes. Add garlic and sun-dried tomatoes and cook for another 2 minutes. Remove the pan from heat and mix in the piñons, bread crumbs, and parsley. Season with salt and pepper. Set aside to cool.

Trim off any silver skin and excess fat on the outside of the roast. Make a pocket by slicing lengthwise down the meat and cutting about two-thirds of the way through. Spoon the reserved stuffing into the slit in the roast, then wrap with kitchen twine to seal the pocket.

Rub the tenderloin with about 3 tablespoons of olive oil, then sprinkle with salt and pepper.

Heat a frying pan over high heat. Add the remaining olive oil, then the roast. Sear the meat on all sides, turning with a pair of tongs.

Place the tenderloin in the prepared roasting pan and place it in the oven. After 15 minutes, lower the oven temperature to 350 degrees F and cook for another 20 minutes or until an instant-read thermometer registers 145 degrees F. Remove the tenderloin from the oven. Let it rest for about 15 minutes before slicing.

Pecan-Cranberry Pork Roast

xxxxxx

I much prefer the pork loin over tenderloin, which tends to be dry and to lack the flavor of the larger cuts of meat.

Preheat the oven to 350 degrees F. Prepare a roasting pan by coating it with cooking spray or lining with aluminum foil.

Make a slit lengthwise in the roast, about three-quarters of the way through and three-quarters lengthwise.

In a medium frying pan, melt the butter over medium heat. Add the green onion and celery and sauté until tender. Add the bread crumbs and mix to combine. Remove from heat, then add the cranberries and pecans, and set aside.

Open the slit in the roast to form a pocket and season the inside and outside with salt and pepper. Fill the pocket with the stuffing mixture. Tie the roast with kitchen twine to keep the pocket closed. Place the roast in the prepared roasting pan and cook for about 1½ hours, or until an instant-read thermometer inserted into the meat registers 145 degrees F.

Let it rest for 15 minutes before slicing.

Serves 10–12

Cooking spray (optional)

1 pork loin, about 8 pounds

½ stick (4 tablespoons) unsalted butter

1 cup sliced green onions

1 cup sliced celery

2 cups unseasoned bread crumbs

12 ounces dried cranberries

12 ounces chopped pecans

1 teaspoon salt

1 teaspoon freshly ground pepper

Pistachio Pork Chops

xxxxxx

Serves 4

Substitute piñons or pecans if you wish, but the pistachios give a nice color to the chops.

6 tablespoons all-purpose flour

½ teaspoon salt

½ teaspoon pepper

1 teaspoon lemon zest

4 boneless pork loin chops, about 4 ounces each

½ stick (4 tablespoons) unsalted butter

2 tablespoons lemon juice

4 tablespoons (¼ cup) honey

4 tablespoons (¼ cup) Dijon mustard

½ cup pistachios, toasted and chopped (see page 11)

In a shallow bowl, combine the flour, salt, pepper, and lemon zest. Place one pork chop in the flour mixture and turn to coat it. Repeat with the remaining chops.

Melt the butter in a large frying pan over medium-high heat. Place the chops in the pan in a single layer and cook for about 7 minutes. Turn them over, then cook for another 5 minutes or until an instant-read thermometer inserted into the center of a chop reads 145 degrees F. Remove and place on a plate. Tent with aluminum foil to keep the chops warm.

To the frying pan, add the lemon juice and scrape up any bits of meat from the bottom of the pan. Add the honey, mustard, and pistachios, stirring until hot. Serve the sauce over the pork chops.

Pecan-Crusted Shrimp

xxxxxx

Serves 4

Cooking spray (optional)

8 egg whites

1 cup honey

1 teaspoon salt

1 teaspoon ground white pepper

24 jumbo shrimp, peeled and deveined, with tails left on

3 cups finely ground pecans (sometimes called "pecan meal")

For this main-course showstopper, buy the largest shrimp you can afford. While the recipe will work with any size shrimp, the larger they are, the fewer you will need to handle.

Preheat oven to 350 degrees F. Line a baking sheet with parchment paper or coat it with cooking spray.

In a mixing bowl, whisk together the egg whites, honey, salt, and pepper until blended.

Split the shrimp down their backs, but don't cut all the way through. Open up the halves to form "butterflies" and press them flat with the palm of your hand.

Place the ground pecans on a flat dish or sheet of parchment paper.

Dip each shrimp into the egg wash, letting any excess drain back into the bowl. Press the shrimp lightly into the pecans, turning to coat both sides. Place shrimp on the prepared baking sheet, arranging them evenly with about 1 inch left around each one.

Place in the oven and bake for 8–10 minutes or just until the shrimp turn pink and are firm to the touch. Overcooking will make the shrimp tough. Remove the tails before eating.

Pan-Roasted Salmon with Pistachios

xxxxxx

Try substituting the same amount of finely chopped pecans for the pistachios for a different taste. A cast-iron skillet works perfectly for this recipe.

Preheat the oven to 400 degrees F.

Place the milk and salmon in a gallon-size plastic bag. Set aside for 10 minutes, then drain milk.

In a shallow baking dish, combine pistachios, flour, brown sugar, salt, and pepper. Place a salmon fillet in the nut mixture, then turn over to coat evenly on all sides.

Heat the oil over medium-high heat in an ovenproof skillet large enough to hold the fillets in one layer. When oil is hot but not smoking, add the salmon. Sear until brown, then carefully turn each fillet over and repeat. Place skillet in preheated oven and bake for 5–8 minutes, just until the fish is done and flakes easily with a fork.

Serves 4

2 cups milk

4 salmon fillets, about 6 ounces each

1 cup finely chopped pistachios

$1/2$ cup all-purpose flour

$1/4$ cup light brown sugar

1 teaspoon salt

2 teaspoons freshly ground pepper

$1/4$ cup canola or vegetable oil

Pecan Catfish

xxxxxx

Serves 4

3/4 cup all-purpose flour

3/4 cup yellow cornmeal

2 cups ground pecans

1 tablespoon sweet paprika

2 teaspoons salt

2 teaspoons ground white pepper

1 teaspoon dry mustard

3 eggs

1 cup buttermilk

4 skinless catfish fillets

1 stick (1/2 cup) unsalted butter

Ground pecans are sometimes available where nuts are sold and are labeled "pecan meal." It's a great shortcut and usually less expensive than buying pecan halves and grinding them.

In a shallow pan, blend the flour, cornmeal, pecans, paprika, salt, pepper, and mustard.

In a wide bowl, whisk together the eggs and buttermilk until well mixed.

Dip each catfish fillet into the egg-buttermilk mixture, then place it in the breading mixture. Turn to coat both sides evenly.

In a large frying pan, melt the butter over medium-high heat. Test the heat by placing a pinch of the breading mixture in the pan. If it sizzles, it's ready. Place the fillets in a single layer in the hot pan and cook for about 5 minutes. Carefully turn over and cook for another 3 minutes, or until the fish is done. It will be firm and, when cut open, will flake easily.

Green Beans with Pecans

xxxxxx

Precook the green beans by adding them to a pot of boiling, salted water. Cook for 2–5 minutes, depending on how thick the beans are, just until crisp-tender. Drain and plunge beans into a bowl of ice water to stop the cooking.

In a large frying pan over medium-high heat, cook the bacon until crisp. Remove from the pan and let it drain until it is cool enough to chop into small dice. In the pan with the bacon fat, add the garlic and sauté for about a minute. Add the pecans, green beans, and reserved chopped bacon and cook just until heated through. Season with salt and pepper to taste.

Serves 4

2 slices thick-cut bacon, preferably applewood-smoked

2 large cloves garlic, minced

1/2 cup pecans, toasted and chopped (see page 11)

1 pound green beans, trimmed and parboiled

1/2 teaspoon salt

1 teaspoon freshly ground pepper

Piñon-Garlic Spinach

xxxxxx

Serves 6

3 pounds baby spinach

1 tablespoon olive oil

1/4 cup piñons, toasted (see page 11)

3 cloves garlic, minced

1/2 teaspoon salt

1 teaspoon freshly ground pepper

Blanching the spinach before sautéing makes it much easier to handle. Just make sure it is well drained before adding it to the hot skillet.

Boil some water in a large kettle or stockpot. Add the spinach and blanch for about a minute. Drain. Place the spinach on a bed of paper towels and lightly squeeze out the excess water.

Heat the oil in a large frying pan over medium-high heat. Add the spinach, piñons, and garlic and cook for about 2 minutes. Season with salt and pepper to taste.

Zucchini-Pecan Sauté

xxxxxx

Serves 2–3

3 tablespoons unsalted butter, divided

1/2 cup chopped pecans

1 pound zucchini, thinly sliced

1/4 cup shredded Parmigiano-Reggiano cheese

Even two zucchini plants produce more squash than my family can eat in one summer! But this dish is quick to make and pairs well with grilled meats or pasta.

In a large frying pan, melt 1 tablespoon of the butter over medium heat. Add the pecans and cook, stirring often, until toasted. Remove the pecans with a slotted spoon and set aside.

Add the remaining butter to the pan and let it melt. Add the zucchini and cook, stirring often, until soft. Toss with the pecans and cheese. Remove from heat and serve.

Broccoli with Orange-Pecan Butter

xxxxxx

Rich, buttery pecans accent fresh broccoli and add a boost of antioxidants to this already nutrient-packed green vegetable.

Serves 6

1 package (about 28 ounces) broccoli florets

2 tablespoons unsalted butter

1 cup pecans, chopped

$1/4$ cup cornstarch

1 cup chicken broth

$1/2$ cup orange juice

2 tablespoons sugar

2 teaspoons orange zest

Steam the broccoli until just tender and keep warm on a serving dish.

In a small frying pan over medium-high heat, melt the butter. Add the pecans and sauté until toasted. Set aside.

In a small saucepan over medium heat, whisk together the cornstarch, chicken broth, and orange juice. Cook, stirring constantly, until the sauce thickens. Add the sugar and orange zest.

Spoon the sauce over the broccoli and sprinkle with toasted pecans.

Sweet and Spicy Pistachio Carrots

xxxxxx

Serves 8

I don't know which is more appealing about this side dish: the flavors or the colors.

2 pounds baby carrots

¹/₂ cup water

¹/₂ stick (4 tablespoons) unsalted butter

¹/₂ teaspoon cayenne powder

¹/₂ teaspoon salt

¹/₄ teaspoon cumin

¹/₄ cup maple syrup

1 cup pistachios, toasted and coarsely chopped (see page 11)

In a large saucepan, combine the carrots, water, butter, cayenne, salt, and cumin. Over high heat, bring the mixture to a boil. Reduce the heat to medium and cover partially with a lid. Simmer until the carrots are tender, about 5–10 minutes, depending on the size of the carrots. The liquid should be reduced to half. Stir in the maple syrup and bring back to a boil. Stir occasionally until the carrots are glazed, about 10 minutes. In the last minute or so of cooking, add the pistachios. Serve hot.

Roasted Asparagus with Piñons

xxxxxx

Serves 4

½ stick (4 tablespoons) unsalted butter, divided

1 pound asparagus, woody ends trimmed

¼ cup water

½ cup grated Gruyère or other Swiss cheese

¼ cup piñons

Salt

Freshly ground pepper

A large cast-iron frying pan can go from stovetop to oven and is a great helper for this recipe.

Preheat the oven to 350 degrees F.

In a large oven-proof frying pan, melt 2 tablespoons of butter over medium heat. Add asparagus in one layer, then pour water over and turn up the heat to medium high. Cover the pan with a lid or aluminum foil and let the asparagus steam for about 3 minutes. Remove from heat and drain off any remaining liquid. Top the asparagus with cheese and sprinkle with piñons. Dot with the remaining 2 tablespoons of butter. Season to taste with salt and pepper. Place the pan in the oven and bake, uncovered, just until the cheese is melted, about 5 minutes.

Roasted Acorn Squash with Maple-Pecan Sauce

xxxxxx

You can start this side dish ahead by preparing the recipe up through roasting the squash. Cover and refrigerate. Thirty minutes before serving, make the sauce and finish baking.

Preheat the oven to 350 degrees F. Coat a 9 x 13-inch baking pan with cooking spray or line with aluminum foil.

Cut the squash in half lengthwise and remove the seeds. Cut the halves crosswise into slices about 1 inch thick. Arrange the slices in the prepared pan and cover with foil. Roast for about 30 minutes.

In a small saucepan over medium heat, melt the butter. Add the brown sugar, maple syrup, and pecans. Cook, stirring often, until the sugar melts.

Remove pan from the oven and uncover. Spoon sauce over the squash and return to the oven, uncovered. Bake for 10–15 minutes, until the squash is tender, basting occasionally with the sauce.

Serves 4

Cooking spray (optional)

2 acorn squash

$1/2$ stick (4 tablespoons) unsalted butter

$1/4$ cup brown sugar

2 tablespoons pure maple syrup

$1/4$ cup chopped pecans

Sweet Potato Mash with Pecans

xxxxxx

Serves 4

This sweet side dish pairs beautifully with any kind of poultry, making it an ideal holiday offering.

3 medium sweet potatoes, peeled and cut into chunks

3 tablespoons unsalted butter

$1/2$ cup chopped pecans

3 tablespoons brown sugar

$1/4$ cup bourbon

$1/2$ cup orange juice

$1/4$ teaspoon freshly grated nutmeg

Salt and freshly ground pepper

In a large saucepan, boil the sweet potatoes in water over medium-high heat until very tender, about 10–12 minutes. Drain and set aside.

In a small saucepan over medium heat, melt the butter. Add the pecans and sauté for about 2 minutes or until toasted. Add the brown sugar and cook until it is melted into the sauce. Add the bourbon and continue to cook for 1 minute. Add orange juice and cook until heated through.

Pour the sauce over the sweet potatoes in a large saucepan. Mash, adding nutmeg, salt, and pepper to taste.

Pistachio Pilaf

xxxxxx

You can experiment with different nuts in this recipe. Pecans or piñons would work equally well with these flavors.

Preheat the oven to 325 degrees F.

Melt the butter in an ovenproof Dutch oven over medium heat. Add the mushrooms, green onions, and garlic. Sauté until tender, about 5 minutes. Add the rice and cook, stirring constantly, for an additional 3 minutes. Stir in the thyme, salt, and pepper. Add the broth, turn up the heat, and bring to a boil.

Remove the pan from the heat; cover. Place in the oven for 40 minutes or until the rice is tender. Stir in the toasted pistachios and serve.

Serves 8

3 tablespoons unsalted butter

1 cup button mushrooms, sliced

$1/2$ cup sliced green onions, green tops only

1 garlic clove, minced

2 cups uncooked white rice

1 teaspoon fresh thyme leaves or $1/2$ teaspoon dried thyme

1 teaspoon salt

$1/4$ teaspoon freshly ground pepper

4 cups chicken broth

$3/4$ cup toasted chopped pistachios (see page 11)

Piñon Orzo with Feta

xxxxxx

Serves 8

1 pound orzo

1/4 cup olive oil

2 tablespoons
unsalted butter

1 clove garlic, minced

1 teaspoon chopped fresh
basil or 1/2 teaspoon dried

1/2 teaspoon crushed red
pepper flakes

1 cup piñons

2 tablespoons
balsamic vinegar

1 cup crumbled feta cheese

Salt and freshly
ground pepper

1 small Roma
tomato, chopped

Orzo is a rice-shaped pasta that makes an elegant side dish. It can be treated like a pilaf and seasoned with nuts and dried fruits.

Bring a large pot of salted water to a boil. Add the orzo and cook until al dente, about 8 minutes. Drain and set aside.

In a large skillet over medium-high heat, place olive oil and butter. Stir in the garlic, basil, and red pepper flakes, then reduce the heat to medium. Stir in the piñons and cook until toasted, about 2 minutes. Remove from heat and stir in the vinegar, cheese, and orzo. Season to taste with salt and pepper. Garnish with chopped tomato and serve.

Pecan-Orange French Toast

xxxxxx

Here is a breakfast entrée you can prepare the night before. In the morning, remove from the refrigerator, preheat the oven, and bake. The recipe can be doubled or tripled to serve a crowd.

In a mixing bowl, whisk together the eggs, ⅔ cup orange juice, milk, ¼ cup sugar, vanilla, and nutmeg. Arrange bread in a single layer in a large, shallow dish. Pour egg mixture over the top. Cover with plastic wrap and refrigerate for at least 2 hours or overnight.

Preheat the oven to 350 degrees F.

Melt the ½ stick of butter in a baking pan large enough to hold all the bread in a single layer. Carefully lift the bread slices out of the custard mixture and arrange in the baking pan on top of the melted butter. Bake for 20 minutes, then remove from the oven. Sprinkle with pecans and bake for an additional 10 minutes.

While the French toast is baking, combine the remaining orange juice and sugar with the 1 stick of butter in a small saucepan. Cook over medium heat until the sugar is melted, but do not boil. Serve this warm over the French toast.

Serves 4

4 eggs

1²/₃ cup orange juice, divided

¹/₃ cup whole milk

³/₄ cup sugar, divided

¹/₂ teaspoon vanilla extract

¹/₄ teaspoon ground nutmeg

8 bread slices, about ¹/₂ inch thick

¹/₂ stick (4 tablespoons) unsalted butter

¹/₂ cup chopped pecans

1 stick (¹/₂ cup) unsalted butter

Pistachio Muffins

xxxxx

Serves 12

Cooking spray

1 cup unbleached
all-purpose flour

1 cup whole wheat
pastry flour

³/₄ cup sugar

2 teaspoons baking powder

¹/₄ teaspoon baking soda

¹/₄ teaspoon salt

³/₄ teaspoon
ground cinnamon

1 teaspoon lemon zest

1 cup miniature
chocolate chips

1 cup coarsely chopped
pistachios, divided

1 cup milk

1 stick (¹/₂ cup)
unsalted butter, melted

1 egg

1 teaspoon vanilla extract

Whole grains and pistachios add fiber to these delicious muffins. To make ahead: bake and freeze, individually wrapped in sandwich bags.

Preheat the oven to 375 degrees F.

Fill a muffin tin with paper liners. Coat the paper liners with cooking spray.

In a large mixing bowl, combine the all-purpose and whole wheat flours, sugar, baking powder, baking soda, salt, cinnamon, and lemon zest. Add the chocolate chips and ¾ cup of the pistachios to the dry ingredients, stirring well to combine.

In a small mixing bowl, whisk together the milk, butter, egg, and vanilla. Add to the dry ingredients and stir just until moistened. The batter will be lumpy. Spoon it into the muffin liners and top with the remaining ¼ cup of pistachios. Bake for 20–25 minutes or until done. Muffins will be golden brown and a toothpick inserted into the center of a muffin will have a few crumbs clinging to it when removed.

Three-Nut Granola

xxxxxx

This granola is a nutritional powerhouse—and it tastes good, too! You can find flaxseed oil in most supermarkets and natural food stores, shelved with the vitamins and nutritional supplements.

Line a large-rimmed baking sheet with parchment paper or coat with cooking spray.

Combine the sugar and cider or juice in a large frying pan set over medium-high heat. Cook, stirring often, for 3 minutes or until the sugar is completely dissolved. Stir in the oats and remaining ingredients and continue to cook for another 5 minutes or until the granola is lightly browned. Turn out onto the prepared baking sheet and let it cool completely. Break into small pieces and store in an airtight container.

Serves 10

Cooking spray (optional)

$2/3$ cup brown sugar

$1/4$ cup apple cider or juice

2 cups rolled oats (not instant or quick-cooking)

1 tablespoon flaxseed oil (optional)

$2/3$ cup piñons

$2/3$ cup chopped pistachios

$2/3$ cup chopped pecans

$2/3$ cup Grape-Nuts cereal

$2/3$ cup dried cherries

$2/3$ cup dried cranberries

$1/2$ cup shelled sunflower seeds

$1/4$ cup sesame seeds

$1/2$ teaspoon ground cinnamon

$1/4$ teaspoon ground nutmeg

$1/4$ teaspoon sea salt

Pecan Buttermilk Waffles

xxxxxx

Serves 6

These waffles can make a weekend breakfast or brunch a special occasion.

2 cups all-purpose flour

1 tablespoon baking powder

1 teaspoon baking soda

1 teaspoon salt

4 eggs

2 cups buttermilk

1 stick ($^1/_2$ cup) unsalted butter, melted

Cooking spray (optional)

$^1/_2$ cup finely chopped pecans

Pure maple syrup, to serve

Preheat the waffle iron.

In a mixing bowl, whisk together the flour, baking powder, baking soda, and salt. In another mixing bowl, beat the eggs until light. Add the buttermilk and mix well. Add the liquid ingredients to the dry ingredients and mix until smooth. Stir in melted butter.

Coat the waffle iron with cooking spray or brush it with butter. Sprinkle some pecans onto the waffle iron plate, then pour on about ¾ cup of batter. Bake until the waffle is light brown and crispy. Repeat with the remaining pecans and batter. Serve with pure maple syrup, if desired.

Pistachio-Lemon Bread

xxxxxx

Makes 8–10 slices

Cooking spray

1³/₄ cups all-purpose flour

³/₄ cup sugar

2 teaspoons baking powder

¹/₄ teaspoon salt

1 cup milk

1 egg, beaten

¹/₄ cup canola oil

2 teaspoons lemon zest

3 tablespoons lemon juice, divided

¹/₂ cup coarsely chopped pistachios

1 tablespoon sugar

Nut breads can be made ahead and frozen. Wrap well in plastic wrap, then place inside a freezer bag. Thaw at room temperature while still wrapped.

Preheat the oven to 350 degrees F. Coat an 8 x 4 x 2-inch loaf pan with cooking spray.

In a medium mixing bowl, stir together the flour, ¾ cup sugar, baking powder, and salt. Set aside.

In another medium mixing bowl, combine the milk, egg, canola oil, lemon zest, and 1 tablespoon of the lemon juice. Add the liquid mixture to the dry ingredients and stir just until moistened. The batter will be lumpy. Fold in the pistachios. Pour the batter into the prepared pan and bake for 50 minutes or until a toothpick inserted in the center of the bread comes out clean.

Stir together 2 tablespoons of lemon juice and 1 tablespoon of sugar. As soon as the bread is removed from the oven, brush it with lemon sugar. Cool for about 10 minutes. Remove the bread from the pan and let it cool completely on a wire rack before slicing.

Mom's Pecan Pralines

xxxxxx

Serves 15

These are the holiday classics in our house.

1 cup light brown sugar, packed

1 cup granulated sugar

1 cup pecan halves

2 tablespoons unsalted butter

1/4 cup boiling water

1 teaspoon vanilla extract

Line a baking sheet with parchment paper or with a silicone baking sheet.

Combine the brown sugar, granulated sugar, pecans, and butter in a heavy saucepan. Pour the boiling water over the sugar mixture. Place the pan on a burner set on high. Boil the sugar mixture for 4–5 minutes, stirring just enough to keep the mixture from sticking to the pan. Remove from heat. Add the vanilla, stirring just until mixed. Working quickly, drop by tablespoonfuls onto the prepared pan; the mixture sets up quickly. Let it stand until it is cool. Wrap the pralines individually in plastic wrap or cellophane; store in an airtight container.

Creamy Pralines

xxxxxx

I offer this alternative to Mom's recipe because these pralines are a little creamier and softer in texture. You will need a candy thermometer to get an accurate temperature reading.

Line a baking sheet with parchment paper or with a silicone baking liner.

Combine the brown sugar, granulated sugar, and evaporated milk in a heavy saucepan over medium heat. Cook until the mixture reaches a soft ball stage, 238 degrees F. Remove from the heat and add the vanilla, butter, and pecans. With a wooden spoon, beat the mixture until it is smooth and creamy.

Drop by tablespoonfuls onto the prepared pan. Check the candy after about 10 minutes. If it has not set up, then scrape it all back into the pan and repeat the cooking instructions.

Serves 12

3/4 cup light brown sugar, packed

3/4 cup granulated sugar

1/2 cup evaporated milk

1/2 teaspoon vanilla extract

2 tablespoons unsalted butter

1 cup pecan halves

Pecan Tarts

xxxxxx

These cookies, which taste like tiny pecan pies, were the traditional dessert at an annual fund-raising luncheon and fashion show in my hometown. They make an outstanding tea-time treat as well.

Coat 2 miniature muffin pans or small tartlet molds with cooking spray.

In a small mixing bowl, combine the cream cheese, butter, and flour until smooth. Cover and let chill for 1 hour until dough is firm.

Preheat the oven to 350 degrees F.

With a teaspoon, scoop out 24 balls of dough, each about 1 inch in diameter. Press one dough ball into each section of the muffin pans, leaving an indentation in the middle for the filling.

In a medium mixing bowl, beat together the egg, vanilla, brown sugar, butter, and salt until smooth. Stir in the pecans. Spoon the filling mixture into the dough-lined muffin pans. Place in the oven and bake for about 25 minutes or until the tartlet shells are light golden and the filling is set.

Makes 2 dozen

Cooking spray

3 ounces cream cheese, softened

1 stick ($1/2$ cup) unsalted butter, softened

1 cup all-purpose flour

1 egg

1 teaspoon vanilla extract

$3/4$ cup dark brown sugar, packed

1 tablespoon unsalted butter, softened

Pinch of salt

$2/3$ cup chopped pecans

Piñon Cookies

xxxxxx

Makes 2 dozen

These cookies will remind you of the sugar cookies known as "tea cakes," but with a Southwestern flair.

Cooking spray (optional)

1 can (8 ounces)
almond paste

Preheat the oven to 300 degrees F.

$^1/_2$ cup granulated sugar

$^1/_2$ cup powdered sugar,
plus more for garnish

Line 2 baking sheets with parchment paper or coat them with cooking spray.

$^1/_4$ cup all-purpose flour

2 large egg whites,
lightly beaten

1 cup piñons

In a food processor fitted with the metal blade, place the almond paste, breaking it up into small pieces, along with the granulated sugar, powdered sugar, and flour. Pulse several times until the mixture is finely ground. Add the egg whites a little at a time, just until the dough comes together. You may or may not need all of the egg whites, depending on the moisture content of the almond paste and other ingredients. Remove the blade from the food processor.

Place the piñons in a shallow dish. With a spoon and damp hands, scoop a small amount of dough and roll it around in the piñons until it is lightly coated. Place the cookie on a prepared cookie sheet. Repeat until all the dough is used, placing the cookies about 2 inches apart.

Place the baking sheets in the oven and bake for 20–25 minutes, or until the cookies are firm. Remove the cookies from the sheets using a thin spatula and let them cool on wire racks. Dust with powdered sugar immediately before serving.

Pecan Muffins

xxxxxx

Makes 12

Cooking spray (optional)

1 cup light brown
sugar, packed

$1/2$ cup all-purpose flour

1 cup chopped pecans

$2/3$ cup unsalted
butter, softened

2 eggs, beaten

Muffins freeze well when wrapped in plastic and placed inside a freezer bag. Let them thaw completely in the packaging for the best texture and flavor.

Preheat the oven to 350 degrees F. Coat a muffin pan with cooking spray or fill each indentation with a paper liner.

In a medium mixing bowl, stir together the brown sugar, flour, and pecans. In another bowl, beat the butter and eggs until smooth. Add this mixture to the dry ingredients and stir just until combined. The batter may be lumpy. Spoon into the prepared muffin pan and place in the oven. Bake for 20–25 minutes or until golden brown. Let cool for about 5 minutes, then remove from pans and let cool completely on wire racks.

Chocolate Pistachio Bread

xxxxxx

Chocolate and pistachio make a great flavor combination. This moist bread is more like a cake and will freeze well if you'd like to make it in advance.

Preheat the oven to 350 degrees F.

Coat a 9 x 5 x 3-inch loaf pan with cooking spray.

In a large mixing bowl, cream together the sugar, butter, milk, and egg until smooth. Stir in the flour, cocoa powder, baking powder, salt, pistachios, and chocolate chips. Scrape into the prepared pan using a flexible spatula. Bake for 50–55 minutes, or until a toothpick inserted into the center of the bread comes out clean. Cool 10 minutes. With a knife, loosen the bread from the sides of the pan, then invert onto wire rack. Turn right side up and allow to cool completely before slicing.

Serves 8–10

Cooking spray

$2/3$ cup granulated sugar

1 stick ($1/2$ cup) unsalted butter, melted

$3/4$ cup milk

1 egg

1 $1/2$ cups all-purpose flour

$1/3$ cup natural cocoa powder

2 teaspoons baking powder

$1/4$ teaspoon salt

1 cup chopped pistachios

$1/2$ cup semisweet chocolate chips

Pecan Sandies

xxxxxx

Makes 3 dozen

Cooking spray (optional)

2 sticks (1 cup) unsalted butter, softened

1/4 cup light brown sugar

2 cups all-purpose flour

1/2 teaspoon salt

1 tablespoon water

1 teaspoon vanilla extract

2 cups finely chopped pecans

1/4–1/2 cup powdered sugar

A holiday favorite, these cookies are also wonderful with a cup of hot coffee or tea.

Preheat the oven to 350 degrees F.

Line 2 baking sheets with parchment paper or coat with cooking spray.

In a mixing bowl, cream the butter with an electric mixer until light and creamy. Add the brown sugar and mix until blended together. Slowly add the flour, salt, water, and vanilla and mix until smooth. Fold in the pecans and mix until evenly distributed.

Put about ¼ cup powdered sugar on a small plate. With a tablespoon, scoop out lumps of dough and form into balls. Roll the balls in powdered sugar and place them on the prepared baking sheets. Bake for about 18–20 minutes or until the cookies are light golden in color and firm. Remove from the oven and transfer to wire racks, with a flexible spatula, to cool. Sprinkle with additional powdered sugar.

Pistachio Crisps

xxxxxx

Try these with piñons for a different taste.

Makes 6 dozen

Preheat the oven to 325 degrees F. Line 2 baking sheets with parchment paper or coat with cooking spray.

Cream together the butter and salt, then add ½ cup of the powdered sugar. When completely incorporated and smooth, add the nuts, vanilla, and flour. Mix until combined.

Divide the dough in half and roll out into logs about ½ inch in diameter. Cut into 1½-inch pieces and place on the prepared baking sheets, about 2 inches apart. Bake for 15–18 minutes.

Place the remaining powdered sugar in a small dish. While the cookies are still warm, roll them in powdered sugar, then let them cool on wire racks.

Cooking spray (optional)

2 sticks (1 cup) unsalted butter, softened

$1/_8$ teaspoon salt

1 cup sifted powdered sugar, divided

2 cups chopped pistachios

2 teaspoons vanilla extract

1 $1/_2$ cups all-purpose flour

Red and Green Holiday Fudge

xxxxxx

Makes 16 pieces

2 cups white chocolate chips or chopped baking squares

1 can (14 ounces) sweetened condensed milk

2 teaspoons vanilla extract

Pinch of salt

1/2 cup dried cherries or dried cranberries

1/2 cup pistachios

Experiment with different kinds of nuts and dried fruit to create your own custom fudge.

Line an 8-inch square baking pan with aluminum foil and set aside.

In a microwave-safe bowl, combine the white chocolate and condensed milk. Heat on medium-high to high power in the microwave, stopping every 30 seconds to stir the mixture until the chocolate is melted and smooth. Watch closely, because white chocolate burns easily.

Remove from the microwave and stir in the vanilla, salt, berries, and pistachios. Pour into the prepared pan and chill for several hours. When the fudge is firm, remove it from the pan. Peel off the foil and cut the fudge into small squares. Place the pieces in paper candy cups for gift giving. Store fudge, well wrapped, in the refrigerator until ready to serve.

Cranberry-Pistachio Biscotti

xxxxxx

These twice-baked cookies are delicious for dunking into a cup of hot coffee or tea.

Makes 3 dozen

Preheat the oven to 350 degrees F.

Prepare 2 baking sheets by lining them with parchment paper or coating with cooking spray.

In a large mixing bowl, whisk the 5 eggs and 1 yolk thoroughly with the sugar, then add the vanilla. In another bowl, stir together the flour, baking powder, salt, and cinnamon. Fold the egg-sugar mixture into the dry ingredients. Add the orange zest, cranberries, and pistachios.

Divide the dough in half. Form each half into a 4 x 12-inch log and place them on the baking sheets. Brush each log with egg white. Place in the oven and bake for 25 minutes. Remove the pans from the oven and let them cool.

Turn the oven down to 325 degrees F.

When the logs are cool enough to handle but still warm, slice them crosswise into ¾-inch cookies. Lay each cookie individually on the cookie sheets. Return the sheets to the oven and bake for 10 minutes. Remove from the oven, turn over all the cookies, then return to the oven and bake an additional 5–7 minutes or until the cookies are dry.

Store in an airtight container.

Cooking spray (optional)

5 eggs

1 egg yolk (reserve the white)

2½ cups sugar

1 teaspoon vanilla extract

3½ cups sifted all-purpose flour

1 teaspoon baking powder

½ teaspoon salt

1 teaspoon ground cinnamon

Zest from 1 orange

1½ cups dried cranberries

1½ cups pistachios

1 egg white, lightly beaten

INDEX